Predators Underwater ~ Reef Cuttlefish

Written and Illustrated by Jeff Terry

The two arms of a reef cuttlefish can walk on the sand with their tips while the other six hide its mouth.

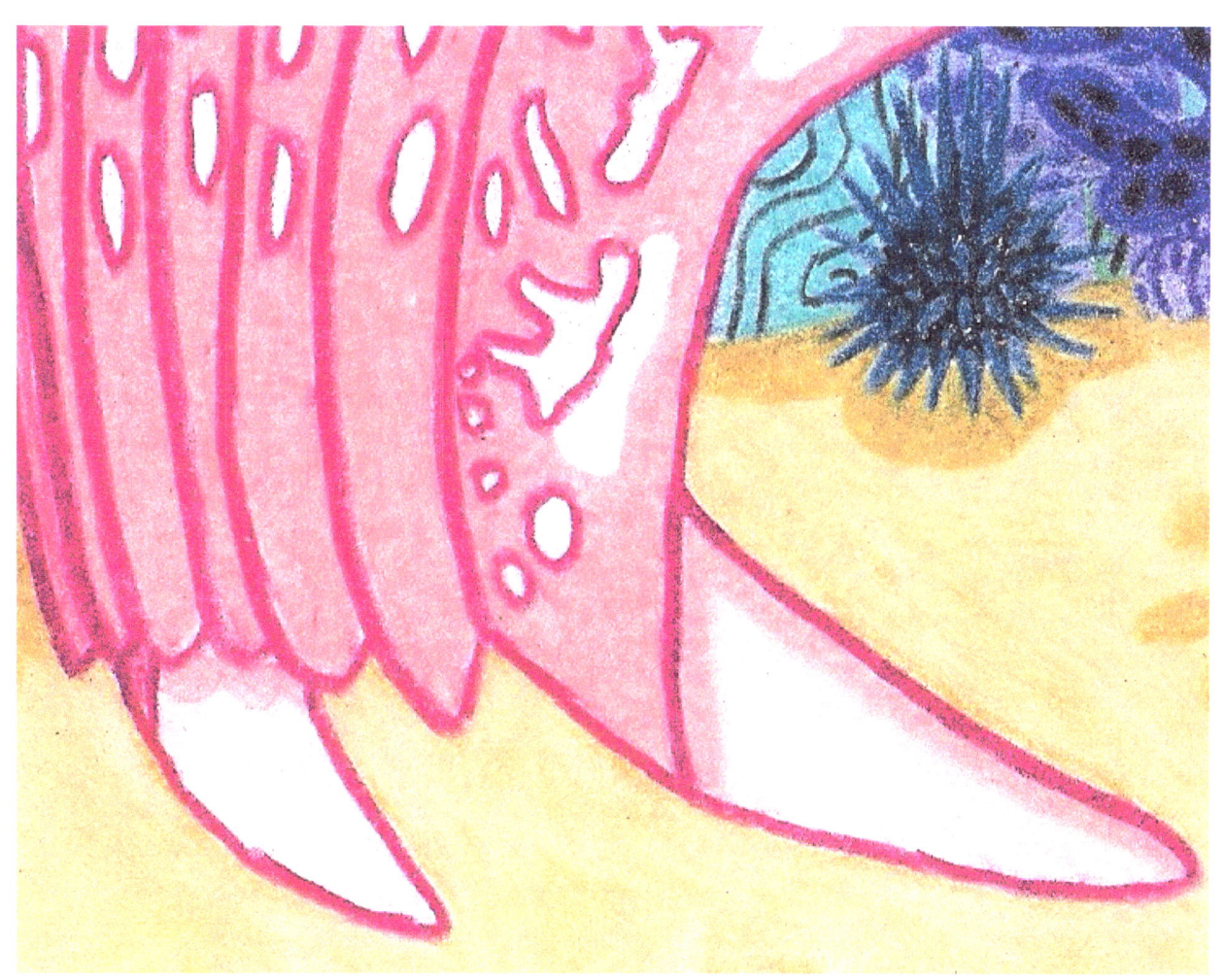

Its two tentacles can nab its prey swiftly and accurately.

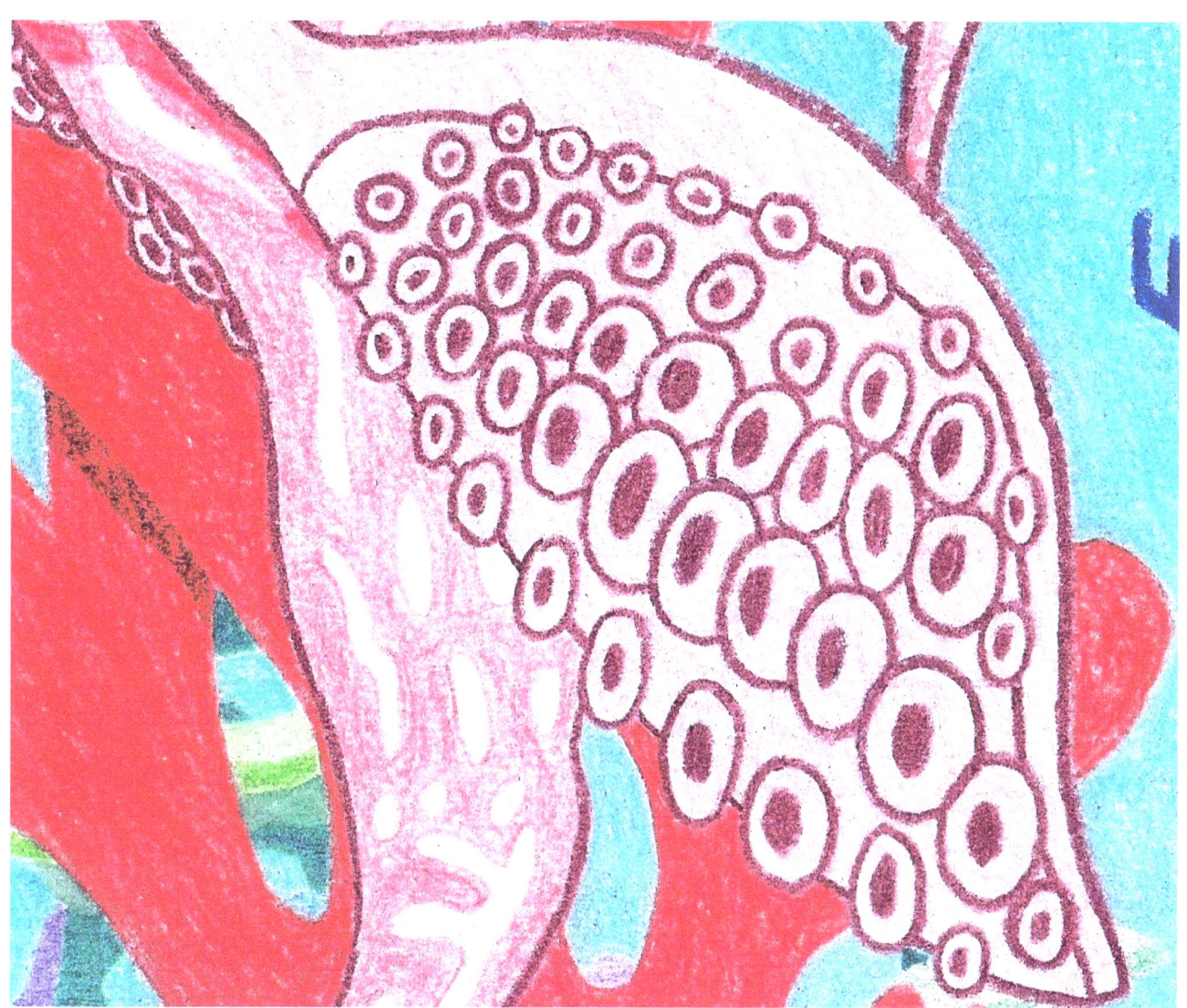

Its beak can scythe up its prey and slobber venom from the inside of its mouth.

Its fins can ripple quickly.

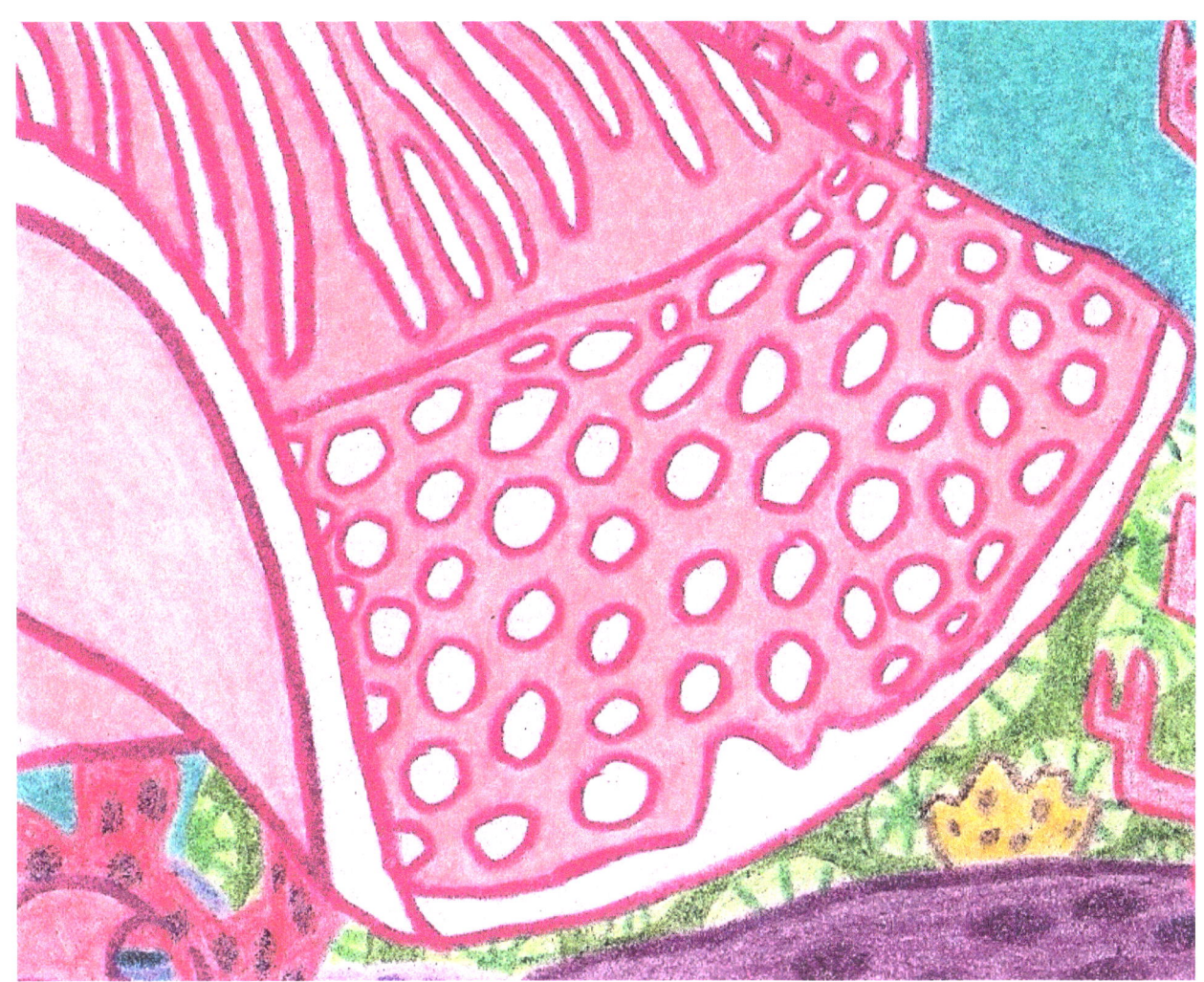

Its mantle can buoy its body with its cuttlebone and its skin can swap colors and morph into part of the coral reef.

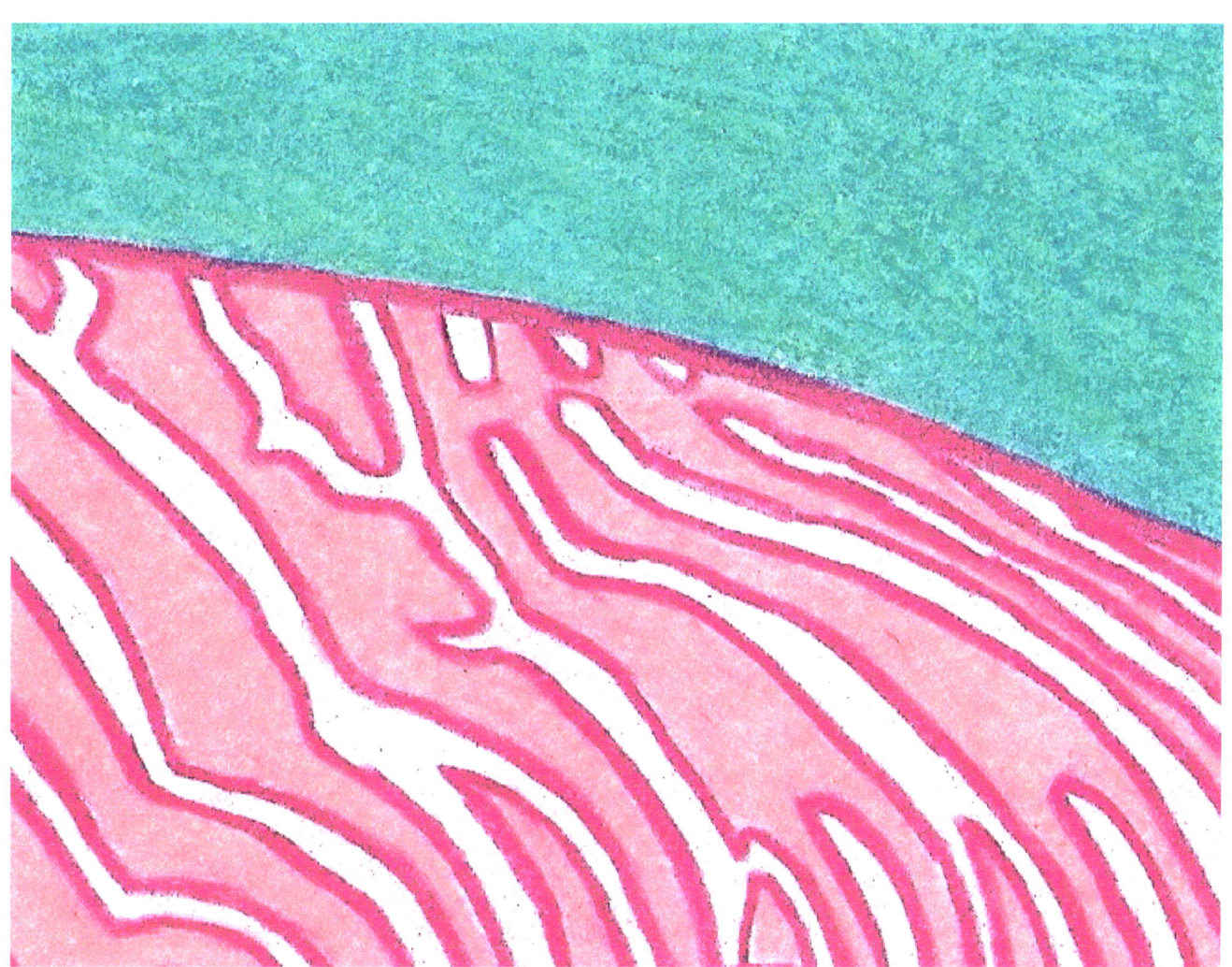

Its funnel can siphon up water and jet it back out.

Its eyes can spy on any prey that move past.

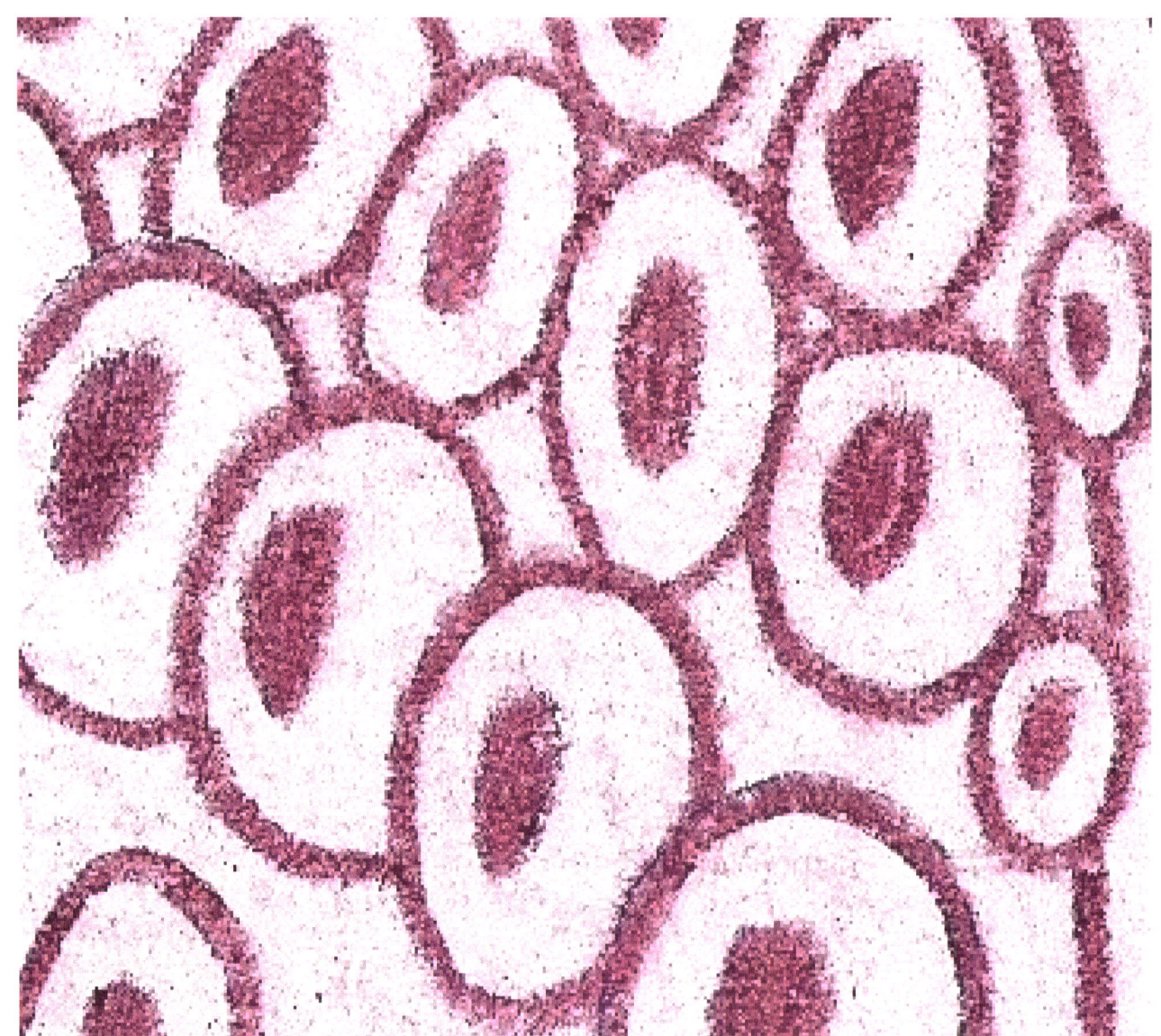

Its suckers can analyze the taste and smell of its prey.

Female cuttlefish can guard their eggs before hatching.

Reef cuttlefish are predators of shrimp and smaller fish.

Jeff Terry enjoys drawing, reading and writing about animals.
"With God all things are possible." Matthew 19:26